Left fielder/First baseman Willie Stargell

THE STORY OF THE PITTSBURGH PIRATES

Pitcher Paul Skenes

THE STORY OF THE

PITTSBURGH PIRATES

JOE TISCHLER

CREATIVE SPORTS

Right fielder Kiki Cuyler

CREATIVE EDUCATION / CREATIVE PAPERBACKS

Published by Creative Education and Creative Paperbacks
P.O. Box 227, Mankato, Minnesota 56002
Creative Education and Creative Paperbacks are imprints of
The Creative Company
www.thecreativecompany.us

Book Design by Wyeth Morgan
Art direction by Blue Design (www.bluedes.com)

Photos By Alamy Stock Photo/Cal Sport Media, 6 (bottom, left); Associated Press/Joe Robbins/Icon Sportswire, cover, John Bazemore, 7 (top, right); Getty Images/Art Rickerby/Time Life Pictures, 18, Bettmann, 9, 10, 20, Diamond Images, 11, Elsa, 7 (top, left), Focus On Sport, 22-23, 26-27, Jamie Squire, 7 (bottom, right), Jared Wickerham, 29, Jonathan Kirn, 6 (top, left), Kidwiler Collection, 10, 16, Leon Halip, 4-5, 32, MLB Photos, 19, National Baseball Hall of Fame Library/MLB, 7 (bottom, left), 12, cover, 15, Nick Cammett/Diamond Images, 30, Rayni Shiring, 2, Rich Pilling, 1, 6 (bottom, right), Rick Stewart, 25, Thearon W. Henderson, 6 (top, right); Wikimedia Commons/National Photo Company Collection, 3, Kansas City Call newspaper (first publication)/public domain, 1, Los Angeles Times, 7 (top, left)

Library of Congress Cataloging-in-Publication Data
Names: Tischler, Joe author
Title: The story of the Pittsburgh Pirates / by Joe Tischler.
Description: Mankato, Minnesota : Creative Education and Creative Paperbacks, [2026] | Series: Creative sports. Major League baseball | Includes index. | Audience: Ages 8-12 | Audience: Grades 4-6 | Summary: "Discover the Pittsburgh Pirates' thrilling journey from early achievements to recent seasons, featuring legendary players, numerous World Series victories, and the Major League Baseball team's passionate fanbase. Written for middle-grade readers. Includes table of contents, sidebars, and index"— Provided by publisher.
Identifiers: LCCN 2025019590 (print) | LCCN 2025019591 (ebook) | ISBN 9798895811054 library binding | ISBN 9798896800583 paperback | ISBN 9798895812310 ebook
Subjects: LCSH: Pittsburgh Pirates (Baseball team—History | Baseball—Pennsylvania—Pittsburgh—History—Juvenile literature
Classification: LCC GV875.P5 T574 2026 (print) | LCC GV875.P5 (ebook) | DDC 796.357/640974886--dc23/eng/20250716
LC record available at https://lccn.loc.gov/2025019590
LC ebook record available at https://lccn.loc.gov/2025019591

Printed in the United States

Shortstop Ronny Cedeno

PITTSBURG

STARGELL
8

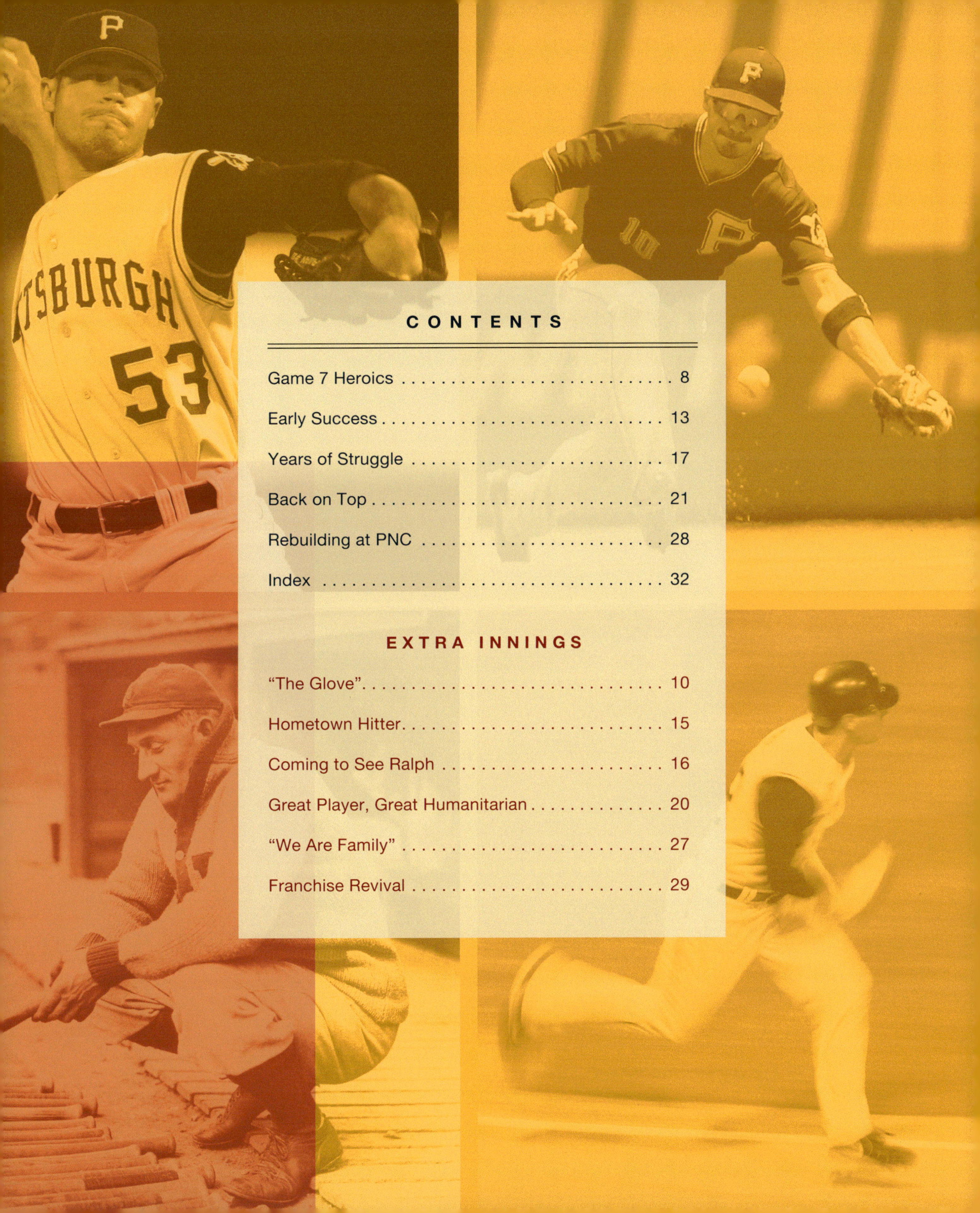

CONTENTS

EXTRA INNINGS

GAME 7 HEROICS

On paper, the 1960 World Series looked like a mismatch. The American League (AL) champions were the New York Yankees. They were no strangers to playing on this big stage. New York had won the World Series 18 times prior to 1960. It had won six titles alone in the 1950s. The National League (NL) champions were the Pittsburgh Pirates. Their success was nearly the opposite of the Yankees. This was Pittsburgh's first World Series appearance in 33 years. Their last World Series title came in 1925.

Despite the disparity in team success, it was Pittsburgh who scored the series' first win. The Pirates took Game 1 on their home field of Forbes Field, 6–4. The Yankees dominated Games 2 and 3 by a combined score of 26–3. Pittsburgh bounced back with two straight low-scoring wins to take a 3–2 series lead. New York easily won Game 6, 12–0, to force a Game 7 in Pittsburgh.

The Pirates had their best pitcher on the mound for Game 7. Vern Law won 20 games in 1960. He was the winning pitcher in Games 1 and 4 this series. Pittsburgh gave Law some

Second baseman Bill Mazerosk

BILL MAZEROSKI
SECOND BASEMAN
PIRATES SEASONS: 1956–72
HEIGHT: 5-FOOT-11
WEIGHT: 183 POUNDS
KEY STATS: 2001 HALL OF FAME INDUCTEE, 10X ALL-STAR, 8X GOLD GLOVE, 2X WORLD SERIES CHAMPION

"THE GLOVE"

Bill Mazeroski was known more for his glove than he was for his bat. Nicknamed "The Glove," Mazeroski would win eight Gold Glove awards over his 17-year Hall of Fame career. Three years he led the league in fielding percentage. He turned 1,706 double plays from his second base position. That is a major-league record. Mazeroski's most memorable play came from his bat. He hit the game-winning home run in Game 7 of the 1960 World Series. Mazeroski remains the only player in history to end a Game 7 of the World Series with a home run. "I was almost at second base when (the ball) finally went over," he said. "Then it took a moment or two to realize what happened – it was gone."

Pitcher Vern Law

early run support. First baseman Rocky Nelson belted a two-run home run in the bottom of the first. The Pirates scored two more in the second to take a 4–0 lead.

Law was keeping Yankees' batters off the bases through four innings. He allowed only two hits. New York finally broke through in the fifth inning on a Bill Skowron lead-off home run. It added four runs in the sixth to take a 5–4 lead. The big shot was a three-run home run from Yogi Berra. Law was replaced after the inning.

It stayed 5–4 until the eighth inning. Johnny Blanchard and Clete Boyer produced run-scoring hits to give New York a 7–4 edge. Pittsburgh erupted in the bottom of the inning. It started the at-bat with three straight singles. Dick Groat delivered a run-scoring single. Later, Roberto Clemente drove in a run with a two-out single to pull the Pirates within a run at 7–6. Hal Smith followed a three-run home run to left to score Groat and Clemente. The Pirates now led 9–7.

The Yankees were not done though. A Mickey Mantle single drove in a run. New York tied the game a batter later. The game went to the bottom of the ninth, tied at 9–9. It would not stay tied much longer. Light-hitting second

baseman Bill Mazeroski led off for Pittsburgh. The first pitch was a ball. The next pitch was launched deep to left, over the wall, for the series-winning home run. The Pirates won 10–9. They were world champions!

How the Pirates won the series is baffling. New York outscored Pittsburgh 55–27 in the series. The Yankees outhit the Pirates, 91–60. Bobby Richardson of the Yankees was named World Series Most Valuable Player (MVP). This marked the only time someone from the losing team earned the honor.

EARLY SUCCESS

Well before Mazeroski's epic home run, the Pittsburgh franchise was part of the American Association. They were a founding member of the new league in 1882. The team was simply listed as "Allegheny" in the standings. The Allegheny River runs through Pittsburgh, Pennsylvania. The franchise moved to the National League in 1887. The team became known as the Pittsburgh Alleghenys. Before the 1890 season, many pro baseball players, including most of the Alleghenys, decided to form their own league. They called it the Players League. It quickly went out of business. NL owners made a rule. Anyone who had gone to the new league was expected to return to the team they were on before. Pittsburgh defied the rule. It signed second baseman Louis Bierbauer. He had been with the Philadelphia Athletics. Angry Athletics officials claimed Pittsburgh stole Bierbauer. "They were no better than pirates," they claimed. Pittsburgh kept their new player. And they adopted the new Pirates nickname, too.

Shortstop Honus Wagner

The Pirates usually finished in the bottom half of the NL until 1900. Then new team president Barney Dreyfuss took over. He added several outstanding players to the roster. The most important addition was shortstop Honus Wagner. In 1900, Wagner led the NL with a .381 batting average, 45 doubles, and 22 triples.

Pittsburgh won three straight NL pennants from 1901 to 1903. They were boosted by Wagner, pitcher Deacon Phillippe, and outfielder and manager Fred Clarke. After winning the 1903 pennant, Dreyfuss put down a challenge. The Boston Americans (later known as the Red Sox) won the AL pennant. Dreyfuss wanted the Pirates and Americans to play in a best-of-nine World Series. The winner would be the true major-league champion. Boston won the series in eight games.

The Pirates were back in the World Series in 1909. They played the Detroit Tigers. Pittsburgh was led by pitcher Babe Adams. He won three games in the series. Now a best-of-seven World Series, Pittsburgh won Game 7, 8–0 to claim their first world championship.

After the title, the Pirates slowly faded. Star pitcher Wilber Cooper provided a few highlights. Outfielder Max Carey was the NL's top base stealer. Pittsburgh's fortunes improved in the early 1920s. Third baseman Pie Traynor joined the team. He solidified the Pirates' defense. He joined Carey and outfielder Kiki Cuyler to give Pittsburgh the top offense in the league. In 1925, the trio led the Pirates to the NL pennant. They faced the Washington Senators in the World Series. Washington jumped out to a 3–1 series lead. But the Pirates stormed back to tie the series. They staged an exciting Game 7 rally against the Senators ace pitcher Walter Johnson. The Pirates captured their second championship!

EXTRA INNINGS

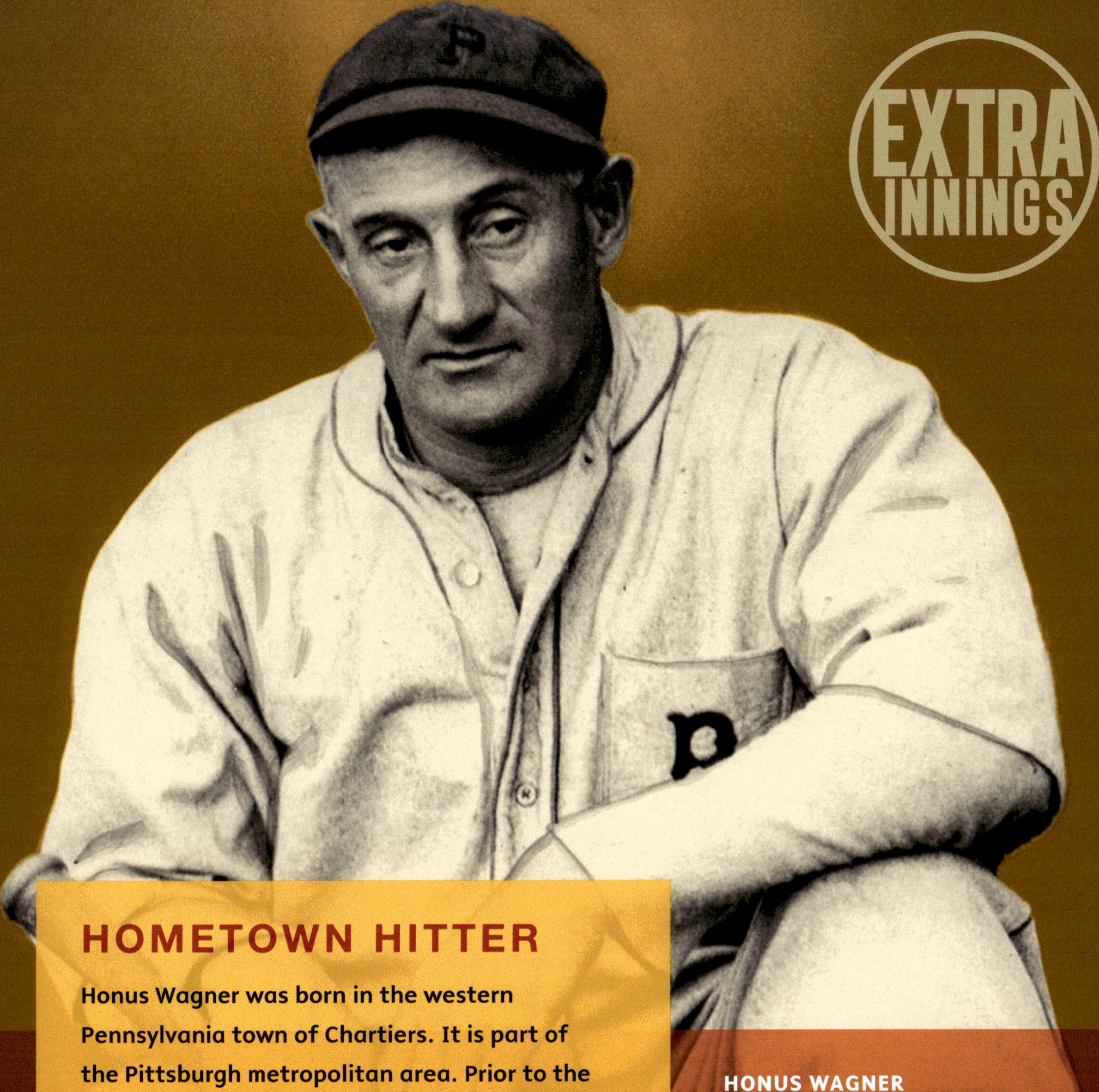

HOMETOWN HITTER

Honus Wagner was born in the western Pennsylvania town of Chartiers. It is part of the Pittsburgh metropolitan area. Prior to the 1900 season, he was traded to his hometown Pirates. That season, he led the NL in batting average for the first time. He hit .381. He kept on hitting throughout the rest of his career. Seven more times, Wagner led the NL in batting. Hall of Fame manager John McGraw called Wagner "The nearest thing to a perfect player no matter where his manager chose to play him." He had the great combination of power and speed. Seven times he led the NL in doubles. Five times he led in stolen bases. Wagner was part of the first induction class to the Baseball Hall of Fame in 1936.

HONUS WAGNER
SHORTSTOP/FIRST BASEMAN/
SECOND BASEMAN
PIRATES SEASONS: 1900–17
HEIGHT: 5-FOOT-11
WEIGHT: 200 POUNDS
KEY STATS: 1936 HALL OF FAME INDUCTEE, 8X BATTING CHAMPION, .328 CAREER BATTING AVERAGE, WORLD SERIES CHAMPION

RALPH KINER
LEFT FIELDER
PIRATES SEASONS: 1946–53
HEIGHT: 6-FOOT-2
WEIGHT: 195 POUNDS
KEY STATS: 1975 HALL OF FAME INDUCTEE, 6X ALL-STAR, 7X NL HOME RUN LEADER, 369 CAREER HOME RUNS

COMING TO SEE RALPH

Ralph Kiner played seven complete seasons in Pittsburgh. He led the NL in home runs each of those years. He was the first NL slugger to record two 50-home run seasons. Kiner played for weak Pittsburgh teams. Still, he thrilled fans every time he stepped to the plate. "The only reason people went to Pirates games was to see him play; this was a team that went 42–112 one year," said sports analyst Ed Randall. "They would be losing 9–2, but the fans would stay to the end to watch him get one more at bat."

YEARS OF STRUGGLE

Following their 1925 title, the Pirates added two more weapons to their already explosive offensive lineup. In 1926, rookie right fielder Paul Waner did two things for the Pirates. He posted a terrific .336 batting average. He also told the team's owner, "My younger brother Lloyd is an even better player than I am. You'd better grab him." Luckily, the Pirates took his advice. For the next decade, the Waner brothers were the heart of Pittsburgh's offense. Each brother weighed only around 150 pounds. Still, they earned the nicknames "Big Poison" and "Little Poison." Fans said they were murder on opposing pitchers. Each was inducted into the Hall of Fame.

Pie and the Poisons led the Pirates to another pennant in 1927. Pittsburgh faced the Yankees in the World Series. But the Pirates were no match for New York's legendary "Murderers' Row" lineup. The Yankees swept the series in four games.

The Pirates remained on the hunt for another NL pennant throughout the rest of the 1920s and '30s. But they could not reach higher than second place. Fans continued to hope for another championship as they cheered for several outstanding performers. Among the best players during those seasons was shortstop Arky Vaughan. He arrived in 1932. He batted .300 or better in each of his ten seasons in Pittsburgh.

Despite their talent, the Pirates fell short year after year. "Gee that was tough to take," Paul Waner later said. "We had good teams, too. You know, Pie, Arky, and me and Lloyd—all good players. But we never quite made it. It'd just tear you apart."

Pitcher Roy Face

During the 1940s, the Pirates struggled. They had just one real star—slugging outfielder Ralph Kiner. He won the NL home run crown seven seasons in a row with his swashbuckling swing. But even Kiner's long balls couldn't keep the team from spiraling downhill. The Pirates lost more than 100 games from 1952 to 1954.

General manager Branch Rickey had a rebuilding plan. He began trading away veterans. He brought in talented young players. They included shortstop Dick Groat and relief pitcher Roy Face. Slugging first baseman Dick Stuart also joined the team. Before the 1955 season, Rickey signed a young Puerto Rican outfielder, Roberto Clemente. He would be the team's brightest star for the next 18 years.

Right fielder Roberto Clemente

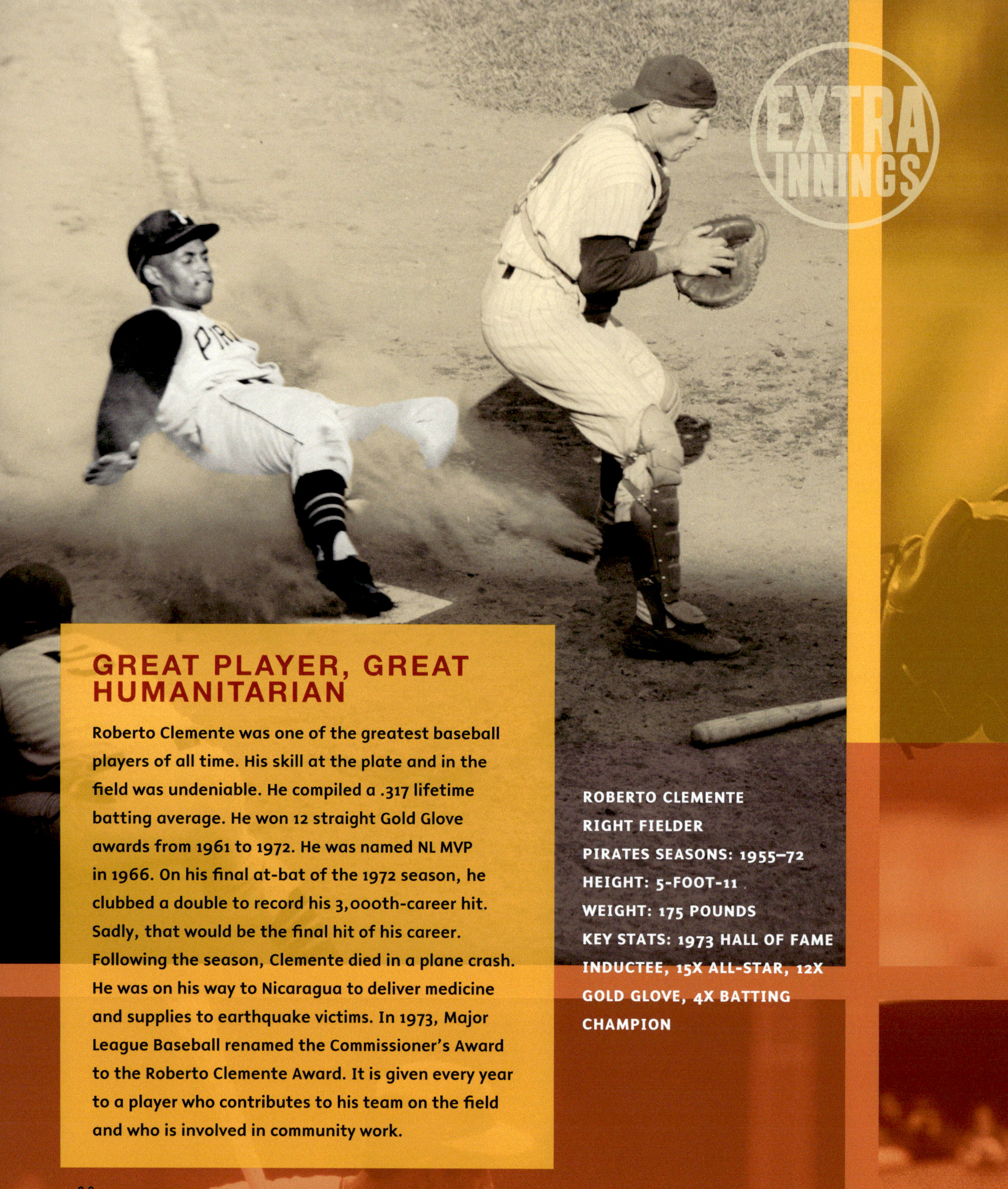

GREAT PLAYER, GREAT HUMANITARIAN

Roberto Clemente was one of the greatest baseball players of all time. His skill at the plate and in the field was undeniable. He compiled a .317 lifetime batting average. He won 12 straight Gold Glove awards from 1961 to 1972. He was named NL MVP in 1966. On his final at-bat of the 1972 season, he clubbed a double to record his 3,000th-career hit. Sadly, that would be the final hit of his career. Following the season, Clemente died in a plane crash. He was on his way to Nicaragua to deliver medicine and supplies to earthquake victims. In 1973, Major League Baseball renamed the Commissioner's Award to the Roberto Clemente Award. It is given every year to a player who contributes to his team on the field and who is involved in community work.

ROBERTO CLEMENTE
RIGHT FIELDER
PIRATES SEASONS: 1955–72
HEIGHT: 5-FOOT-11
WEIGHT: 175 POUNDS
KEY STATS: 1973 HALL OF FAME INDUCTEE, 15X ALL-STAR, 12X GOLD GLOVE, 4X BATTING CHAMPION

BACK ON TOP

By 1960, Clemente and the other recruits were in place. They were ready to make another run at the NL pennant. Everything seemed to go right for the Pirates in 1960. The team compiled a 95–59 record. It won the NL by seven games. Groat was named the league's Most Valuable Player (MVP). He led the league in batting with a .325 average. Clemente batted a solid .314. Pitcher Vern Law finished with a 20–9 record. He won the NL Cy Young Award. The Pirates won their first World Series championship in 35 years thanks to Bill Mazeroski's historic Game 7 walk-off home run.

Pirates teams during the 1960s were fun to watch. Law and Bob Friend led the pitching staff. First baseman Donn Clendenon and outfielder Willie Stargell supplied power. Groat and Mazeroski were a solid double-play combination.

In 1969, divisions were added to the AL and NL. The Pirates were sent to play in the NL East Division. The following season, they won the division. But they lost to the Cincinnati Reds in the NL Championship Series (NLCS).

The 1970s brought a lot of success to the Pirates. They had only one losing season in the decade. They made the playoffs 6 out of 10 seasons. In 1971 and 1979, Pittsburgh won the World Series.

The opponent for both World Series appearances was the Baltimore Orioles. Clemente had a stellar '71 series. He collected 12 hits over the 7 games (.414 batting average). He hit a home run in Game 7. The Pirates won 2–1. Clemente was named World Series MVP. Catcher Manny Sanguillen also had a great series. He added 11 hits.

PIRAT
MO

1979 Pittsburgh Pirates celebrate after winning Game Seven of the World Series.

The 1979 World Series also went seven games. Pittsburgh trailed 3 games to 1 in the series. Stellar pitching kept them alive. Jim Rooker and Bert Blyleven combined to allow just six hits as the Pirates won Game 5, 7–1. In Baltimore for Game 6, John Candelaria and Kent Tekulve shut out the Orioles, 4–0. In Game 7, four pitchers combined to allow just four hits. Trailing 1–0 in the sixth, Stargell gave the Pirates the lead with a two-run home run. Pittsburgh added two insurance runs in the ninth. The Pirates won 4–1. They were champions for the second time in the decade and fifth time overall.

The team sank back in the standings following the latest title. In 1986, two talented young outfielders arrived, Barry Bonds and Bobby Bonilla. They spearheaded a turnaround. In 1990, they led the Pirates back to the postseason. More than two million fans packed Three Rivers Stadium that season. They watched Bonds bat his way to the NL MVP award. He smacked 33 home runs and drove in 114 runs. He stole 52 bases. Bonilla was close behind in the MVP voting. Pitcher Doug Drabek won the NL Cy Young Award. He finished with 22 wins. The Reds beat the Pirates in the NLCS.

The Pirates won NL East Division titles again in 1991 and 1992. Both times they came up short against the Atlanta Braves in Game 7 of the NLCS. The Braves shut out the Pirates, 4–0 in Game 7 in 1991. The following year was an excruciating Game 7 defeat at Atlanta. Pittsburgh led 2–0 going into the bottom of the ninth inning. But Atlanta scored three runs to win the series.

Third baseman/outfielder Bobby Bonilla

PIRATES

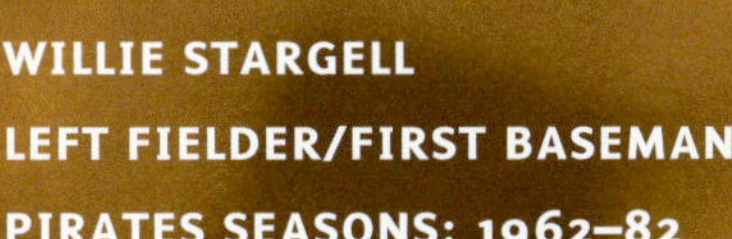

WILLIE STARGELL
LEFT FIELDER/FIRST BASEMAN
PIRATES SEASONS: 1962–82
HEIGHT: 6-FOOT-2
WEIGHT: 188 POUNDS
KEY STATS: 1988 HALL OF FAME INDUCTEE, 7X ALL-STAR, 1979 NL MVP, 475 CAREER HOME RUNS

"WE ARE FAMILY"

Willie Stargell was one of the team's leaders in 1979. He created a close-knit Pirates family. Teammates called him "Pops." He chose a theme song for the team, a disco tune called "We Are Family." He requested that it be played at every home game. "That song not only brought us and the fans closer together," recalled Stargell, "but it became a rallying cry for the city as well. Pittsburghers all moved to the same beat." That beat was a winning one. Pops led his family to victory over the Baltimore Orioles in a thrilling seven-game World Series.

REBUILDING AT PNC

Bonds and Bonilla soon left the club. Wins became hard to come by in Pittsburgh. From 1993 to 2012, the Pirates failed to record one winning season. The 20-straight losing seasons set a major-league record. The team still developed good, young players along the way. The Pirates finished just five games out of first place in the NL Central Division in 1997. The squad was led by second baseman Tony Womack, outfielder Al Martin, and catcher Jason Kendall.

The Pirates played three more seasons at Three Rivers Stadium. In 2001, the Pirates opened PNC Park. It was located on the Allegheny River, near where the franchise's first field stood in the 1880s. PNC Park was new. But it paid homage to the team's history. Fans crossed the Roberto Clemente Bridge to reach the park. Then they passed statues of Clemente, Honus Wagner, Bill Mazeroski, and Willie Stargell located outside the stadium. The new stadium was a hit with fans. But the level of play was not. The team had losing records its first 12 seasons at PNC Park.

By 2006, the Pirates had a promising lineup. Top pitchers included Zach Duke and Ian Snell. All-Star outfielder Jason Bay had been NL Rookie of the Year in 2004. Catcher Ronny Paulino and infielder Freddy Sanchez provided punch. But the team lost 95 games.

The team lost 105 games in 2010. But another young core of talented players was budding. Center fielder Andrew McCutchen had quick bats and speedy legs. He was backed by slugging first baseman Garrett Jones. Second baseman Neil Walker added slick hitting. In 2011, Clint Hurdle was brought on

FRANCHISE REVIVAL

The Pirates were not a very good team when they drafted Andrew McCutchen in the first round of the 2005 MLB Draft. They were in the middle of 20 straight losing seasons. He was called up to the big leagues in 2009. He batted .286 his first season. With McCutchen manning center field, the Pirates soon began winning more games. They went from 62 wins his rookie season to 79 in 2012. He had his best season to date that year. He batted .327 with 31 home runs. The following year, he hit .317 and was named NL MVP. The Pirates recorded their first winning season since 1992. They won 94 games. He helped the Pirates advance to the postseason in 2014 and 2015 as well.

EXTRA INNINGS

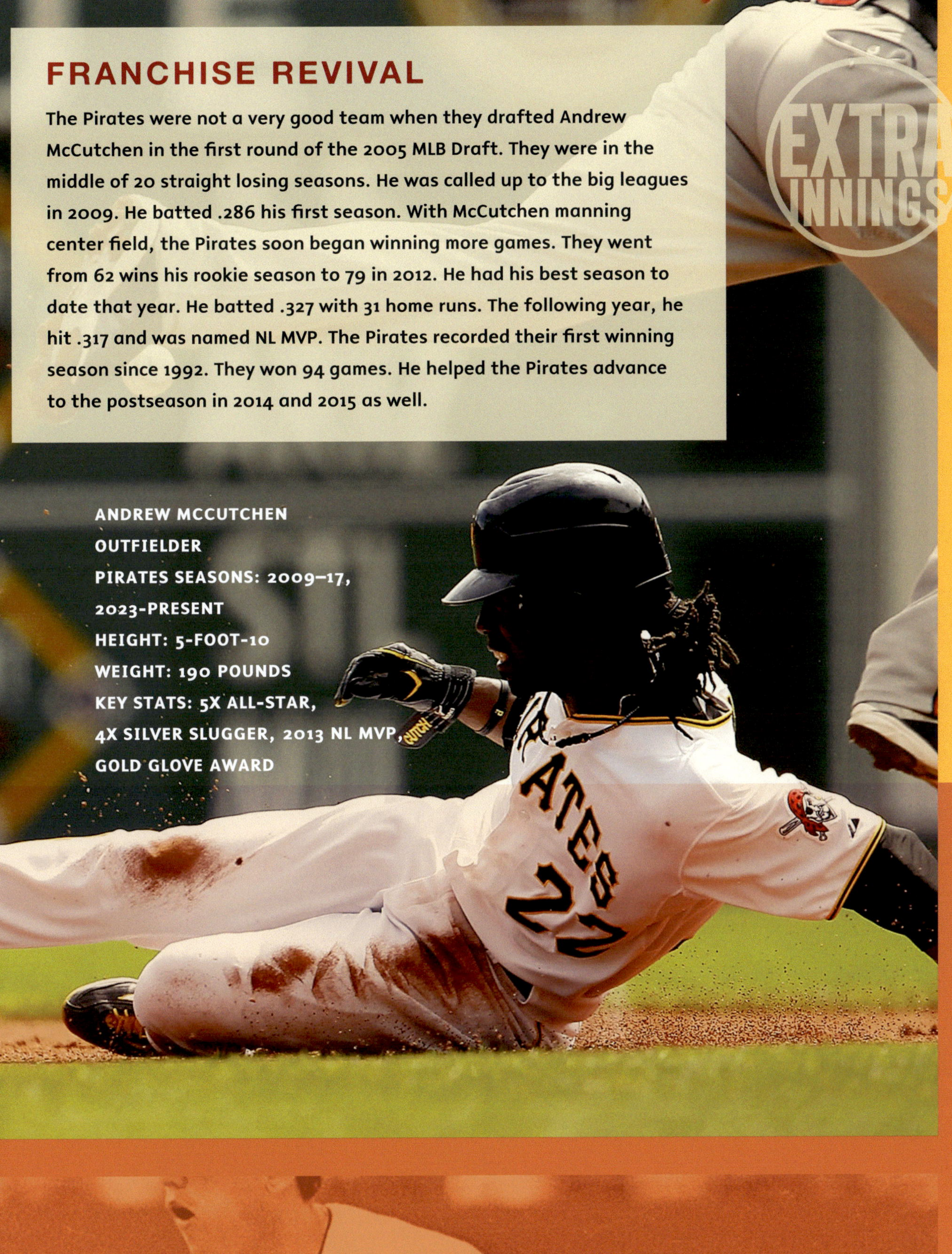

ANDREW MCCUTCHEN
OUTFIELDER
PIRATES SEASONS: 2009–17, 2023-PRESENT
HEIGHT: 5-FOOT-10
WEIGHT: 190 POUNDS
KEY STATS: 5X ALL-STAR, 4X SILVER SLUGGER, 2013 NL MVP, GOLD GLOVE AWARD

SHEETZ

as manager. The new skipper got along well with his players. He also pushed them to succeed.

A turnaround slowly began. In 2013, a record 2.2 million fans poured into PNC Park. They cheered for the first winning Pirates team in two decades. Pittsburgh won 94 games. McCutchen was named NL MVP. Rookie pitcher Gerrit Cole won 10 games. The club earned a postseason berth for the first time since 1992. The Pirates hosted Cincinnati in the NL Wild Card Game (NLWC). Catcher Russell Martin electrified the home crowd with two home runs. Pittsburgh easily won 6–2. The Pirates faced the St. Louis Cardinals in a best-of-five NL Division Series. Pittsburgh took a 2–1 series lead. Cole gave up only one run in a Game 2 win. But the Cardinals won the final two games of the series.

The Pirates reached the postseason again in 2014 and 2015. Both seasons they hosted the NLWC Game. They were shut out by the San Francisco Giants, 8–0, in 2014. The following year, Pittsburgh won 98 games. It had the second-best record in all of baseball. But they finished second in the NL Central behind St. Louis who won 100 games. They hosted the Chicago Cubs in the NLWC Game. Pittsburgh could not generate any offense and lost, 4–0.

After the great three-year stretch, Pittsburgh started reverting back to their losing ways. Cole and McCutchen left after the 2017 season. The team has finished last or next-to-last in the NL Central every year from 2017 to 2024. They won just 19 of 60 games in the COVID-shortened 2020 season. They followed that up with at least 100 losses in 2021 and 2022.

Pittsburgh has promising pitching stars. Paul Skenes had a stellar year in 2024. He went 11–3 with a 1.96 earned run average. He was the easy choice for NL Rookie of the Year. Mitch Keller was an All-Star in 2023. These new stars hope to follow in the footsteps of past Pirates greats and bring another title to Pittsburgh soon.

Third baseman Isiah Kiner-Falefa

INDEX